You Are Entitled…..

By: Benny R. Ferguson Jr.

You are Entitled…

You Are Entitled
By Benny Ferguson © 2014

ISBN:
978-1-7354117-0-5

Published by:
The Ferguson Company

Editor & cover design:
http://roxanec.wix.com/time-to-read.com

Introduction

To paint a picture of what is to come, I want you to think of a tiny chasm, something like a small crack in the earth. It is small, tiny, and insignificant, but if you put your ear to it you can hear the grumblings of the entire earth. An entire planet speaks of its many adventures, its many encounters, its stumbles, its failures and its enormous comebacks.

If you look into it, you can see and feel the countless lives that have been lived, died and returned to the clay. It is the home of lost bodies. It is the collector of the physical machines that we, as human beings, have used for millions of years to claim what is ours, the beauty love and joy that is present and radiant in magnificent glory. It is a gift from mother earth herself.

Sadly, at some point, as we moved down through time, we have forgotten a timeless truth. We have forgotten a truth that rings true in all the ancient wisdoms of the world. A truth that makes living a matter of fact, an indomitable chore to see just how high you can soar, how great you can become in the eyes of your family, in the eyes of your children and your wife, in the eyes of the world, but you have forgotten.

You have forgotten that the earth, this physical existence is your playground. There is nothing that you have to do. There is nothing that you should do.

You do not have to get out of bed in the morning. You do not have to go to work. You do not have to stay married. You do not have to parent your children. I did not say that you shouldn't. I said you do not have to.

Human beings have taken on the false cares of society. Cares that have been implied and given importance, many with business in the background, and with the hustle and bustle of life being the main outward focus, you have become engulfed with all the things that you think you should do and feel that you have to do, and you have

You are Entitled...

forgotten that you have a choice. You have forgotten that you do not have to.

If you are brave enough to take a moment and STOP, and take an objective, honest look at your life and see if you are doing what you feel you must do or if you are doing what you choose to do, I will give you the tools to use from this day forward.

When you look at your life, if you want to make grand improvements or minor changes, complete upheavals or subtle adjustments, you will have the tools to do just that.

My fellow human beings, the answer lies in your name. The answer lies in that which you are being, and nothing more. It is the precept to your life, and if you can take in even a fraction of what is presented in this book, you will be well on your way to drastic changes and to a life not that dreams are made of, but a life that makes dreams a reality.

Benny R. Ferguson Jr.

A Common Thread

First I would like to start off with a clear understanding of the fact, that if you look around the world, at each major religion as presented by an anointed teacher, you will see that they each have pointed you inward to find the Source of your being. This Source is called God, Allah, Brahmin; it is the source of the Tao, and it is that emptiness, that freedom which is sought by the follower of Buddhism. All of these things are the same thing.

It is the mighty wind prayed to by the Native Americans. It is the mighty warrior prayed to by the African tribes.

It is the water that runs slow into the desert, and appears again as ice in the polar ice caps. It is the breath that moves in and out of your body, at a rate beyond your conscious awareness.

It is that which gives intelligence to the seed of the mighty Oak tree. It is the seed of a baby whale.

It is the coming and going of ideas, conflicts and counterfeits in the mind.

It is the comet unseen except at night. It is the brilliant star that glows in the night sky, unmoving, unsheltered.

It is you as you move through your day, making decisions, loving and hating, high and low, and you are it.

There is no separation between you and that which you call God, that which you claim to worship, and this my fellow human beings is the first mental obstacle that you must allow to pass in order to move forward.

Your lack of self-confidence and self-worth all extend from here. Your lack of trust in the world, in the universe all extend from here. Your inability to call forth the resources and abilities that you need to live the life that you desire extend from your lack of understanding, your lack of belief.

You are Entitled…

You are all divine princes and princesses. You have free reign over the riches of the throne, but you must believe it before you can claim it.

Over the top is a less than proper way to describe what has happened to the mind of man. It has become cluttered with ill fates, sickness, and the possibility of death. None of which are etched in stone or declared to be true until you believe them to be, and when you believe them to be you cut off the possibility of any other options, any other possibilities until you observe that they are available through the eyes of another human being.

Courage, this is where you are. It takes courage to turn away from what you normally think. It takes courage to put aside the worries of others until you find yourself. It will take courage to reclaim the throne of your mind, for you have been reduced from royalty to hired hands.

To wrap up this segment, know that you are special, that your mere existence is a gift to the world and that all who come in contact with you will either meet the real you, or a version of you that is a lesser shell. You have been gifted with talent. Whatever you desire to do or be, you have the talent to achieve and to overcome any obstacle. You have a choice, a choice to do everything or to do nothing. You have a choice to be anything or to be nothing. You have the choice to create your destiny or fall victim to the turbulent winds of life. Those winds are the servant and you are the master.

The chosen often falls on the path of regret for to choose and not choose wisely yields a life not lived but spoiled.

All choices are available to you. All experiences are available to you. To choose to do nothing is a grand choice. To choose to do everything, well, that is a grand choice too.

You decide.

What Stops You

To close sharply down to the letter of what stops you in life, you close your eyes and shut off the outside world. Nothing out there stops you. The people that appear in your life are mere flickers in the flame of experience. The events that occur in your life are transient conglomerates of ideas, yours and someone else's who, for a brief time, come together.

What makes a life changing experience? It is an experience that forces you to look inward at your current ideas about life and evaluate what you believe, what you have been taught. If it has never happened to you, it means that you have been playing it safe. It means that you have never pushed the envelope on your life to reach the unexplainable as to why something has not occurred, why you cannot reach that star that you can see clearly and that others seem to reach with ease. What makes you different?

What stops you? When you look inward you find that there is a delicate mix of positive and negative thoughts and emotions that swirl in your being all of the time. You are on a roller coaster of thoughts and feeling, and you do not know how to get off. The circumstances of life reflect this up and down inner ride. Sometimes things are going well, sometimes they are not. Sometimes you are happy and excited; sometimes you are less than jovial. These are the normal patterns for the uninitiated, for the soul who has yet to discover their true worth and power.

As you look inward, in a calm relaxed state you begin to recognize that you have free reign over thoughts. Thoughts come and go, and you can originate thoughts as you choose. You can choose to begin thinking about anyone or anything at any moment. This is a gift and a choice. Your thoughts can be of the grandest, of the most high, or they can be of terrible pain and suffering followed by the accompanying feeling or emotion.

One always follows the other. Feeling always follows the thought. The mental images associated with your thoughts carry the fuel of emotion that gives the images life. This fuel propels the images out into the universe where they grow in strength and number and size until the thoughts or ideas appear, materialize as experience.

This is a constant cycle, an incredible machine that never sleeps, but the key, the turning points are the types of thoughts that you entertain, hold and focus upon in your mind.

You have certain types of thoughts and emotions about relationships. You have certain thoughts and emotions about money. You have certain thoughts and emotions about your health. You have certain thoughts and emotions about your spiritual connection to your source and these thoughts and emotions either propel you forward or they bind you. They serve to connect you or to separate you, but they are fully within your control.

The wisdom text of old states that you must ask for what you want believing that you already have it. This is an act of thinking and feeling now, in the present, in alignment with that which you desire. You cannot desire greater finances, more money, and think, feel, believe in lack, poverty, and scarcity. You cannot believe in health, and think, feel, and perform activities which speak to your belief in illness and disease. You cannot desire loving relationship, and harbor thoughts and emotions of fear and anger of past hurts. The one you focus on is the one that will appear in your life and until the thinking and feeling is changed, its mirror reflection in life will stay the same.

The error most human beings, who have not realized their worth, make is believing that they can have their experience one way in physical reality, while their inner reality is something entirely different. This is a tragic mistake. It completely goes against all the rules of mythology and technology where the person must and always overcome himself or herself first before they triumph and prevail. Even in modern movies, the protagonist almost always has some inner fear, obstacle or block that keeps them from performing, achieving, deciding, or getting the girl. With technology, it is the inner workings of the machine that prevents its successful display of worth on the outside. Computer chips, faulty wirings; these are the things that keep technology from performing or living up to its desired purpose. Everything exists and reigns inwardly before its true purpose and worth is realized outwardly, and the human life is no different.

Common Causes

To date, the common causes of failure and success in the human existence is the detailed belief in the negative energy that exists in the universe. First, all physical and nonphysical matter exists as a part of the intricate makeup of positive and negative energy. On the subatomic level this rings true as every atom in every molecule contains a neutron and a positron in its nucleus, and is balanced out as to its purpose by the tremendous speed and momentum of an electron. This continues even into the deeper realms of existence, and becomes a moot point as the energy and flow of life moves into its wave form as opposed to its particle form.

As it relates to the existence of human beings, the negative and positive energy exists fully, through and through, in the body of every human, and is absolutely necessary to the balance of life. Without this balance there would be no recognition of joy without sorrow. There would be no pleasure without pain. There would be no up without down, and so on and so forth. Opposites exist within the plane of physical reality to allow for choice. Life flows on. The reason and unconscious operation of the body is not yours although you can and always have been able to influence it. Yours is the choice of which energies to align yourself with.

The energy of thought and emotion are generated by you, the individual, and are a choice. Whether you are attracting and living that which is congruent to you is in the feeling, and unless you have begun to lie to yourself and mentally make excuses for the life you presently experience, you merely need to gage your life by your emotions. Emotion and thought go hand in hand. Certain types of emotions follow certain types of thoughts. For simple purposes and understanding we will use the bases of Love and Fear. Love and Fear can both be very powerful allies, but they tend to yield very different results in the end. Love is the coat that warms, builds, encourages, develops and grows all things. It is Love that welcomes the seeds of life, accomplishment and expansion. It is Love that permits the weak to lean on the strong. It is Love that feeds those who have yet to discover their true value and worth. It is Love that discovers the seed of greatness in everyone.

Fear, on the other hand, although it can be a great motivator in the beginning has terrible repercussions. It is fear that destroys, tears down, and stifles. It is fear that clings for fear of loss. It is fear that doesn't recognize abundance. It is fear that hoards the substance that is meant for all. It is fear that holds the commonplace of regret, resentment, and conflict.

These two powerful emotions are the result of a focus of the mind. They reveal the inner nature of the person that wields them, and they reveal the reason for consistent success and/or failure.

The thought of unnatural and unholy ideas yield fear based emotion and this is the start of the downfall of society.

A mind that is guided and directed by the highest of visions and the highest of ideas is always focused and becoming a greater version of itself. A mind that only dwells on ideas pertaining to present circumstances is stagnating, or worse, falling to lower states of mind, of thinking.

To know what this feels like, think of a time or place where everything was perfect, where you had fun, and for a brief time you were without care. Remember the feeling and capture it. To you this is precious because at this moment that feeling has changed your whole perspective on life, on your prospects for the day, on the possibility for you, on the type of people you will meet.

Think of the last time you had a family gathering, say Thanksgiving or Christmas. Imagine if you were capable of taking all of the people you remember being there, aunts, uncles, cousins, brothers, sisters, nephews, nieces, mother, and father. Imagine if you were capable of taking them all out to the finest restaurant without a care for tomorrow.

If you dwell on these types of ideas, the mind begins to formulate ways to achieve and become those things. It begins the work of becoming that type of being because you have sewn the seed. From that point on it is a matter of focus, intention, and belief.

Focus is where you continuously give your attention to the idea. You feed it, so to speak, with positive emotion, and excitement. Rolling it around in your mind as if you are there, seeing everyone's faces, hearing the laughter, sharing the smiles, smelling the food. It's a magnificent feeling.

Intention is expressing the joy that you intend to create. You intend to create an avenue for fellowship in a way that has never been experienced before.

Belief is the foundation on which these ideas are built. You believe yourself to be worthy of the ability to provide. You must believe yourself to be capable of the feeling of wealth for its inevitable materialization to be true for you.

Either way, these ideas must be breathtaking for you in your present position in life, but at the same time seem possible.

Are these the types of ideas that are guiding your life, or ideas of despair, regret and resentment of others? The ideas that you dwell upon are either drawing you to higher states of understanding and conscious, or they are dragging you deeper into the lower states of consciousness and experience.

The Seamless Flight

The seamless flight of the individual human being is one of incremental growth. While at the same time this is not true, because growth is actually exponential but time must be allowed for integration which can sometimes be slow.

But the seamless flight of the individual is one where the ideas of possibility continuously pull a person further and higher. It may be the idea of being a business owner that allows a person to unfold their wings. It may be the idea of beautiful relationship that prompts the unfolding. It may be the observing of someone close that reveals more is possible. Take a look around, see who is attempting to do more. Ask what is different about them from you?

The only difference is that they have had experiences at some time and place that has revealed the presence of their wings. They may not be unfolded, but that individual knows they are there.

The seamless flight is allowed by a mind that is excited about the challenge. You cannot be deterred or shy away from the unknown. The Eagle does not know what dangers await tomorrow when it decides to take flight, but it takes flight anyway because that is its nature.

The unforeseen challenges that lie ahead serve to strengthen your wings. There may be challenges of communication and relationship. There may be challenges of alliance. There may be challenges of narrowing your purpose, refining your mission and your vision. It may be the challenge of realizing you are meant to serve, no matter how successful you become. Any and all challenges that are to be experienced serve to strengthen your wings.

As a former doctor put it, "To fail with one life, is to succeed with another. It's the only way to know what works and what doesn't."

Seamless flight requires some direction even if it is not fully clear. What do you hope to achieve? Where do you intend to go? What do you intend to happen? These are questions that help narrowing your direction, and you follow them. No bird of nature has the ability to take flight, stop in midair and reverse their position. They must continue forward, as you must do.

The decision to fly must be yours. It cannot be forced upon you. This decision opens you up to finding the quiet, hidden voice within you that has been beckoning you for years.

The decision cultivates and begins to gather all of your mental resources, resources that you did not even know you had as you prepare for flight.

Getting off the ground may be the most difficult part. It is the time of the most intense focus and effort. It is the time when you jump from follower of the world to becoming more acutely aware of your inner guidance. It is the time when you draw upon the most valuable resource you have to attend to the details and to carry out the tasks at hand. Remembering that all is necessary for the unfolding of your wings, and that your wings are there.

A Couple of Tidbits

You, my friend, are the awesome of the river, with a force raging under even the current that is visible on the surface. You are the ocean, which makes a living space for the many animals and creatures that relies on you for their survival. To distinguish the monotony from the solitude is what has to take place in order for you to know the true current of power that flows within you.

This current of power is the movement of spirit. It is the movement of your non-physical being. This current is what notions you to do things and when you forget you say, "Something told me to do that." There is nothing insignificant. There is nothing too small. So many bad decisions are made because this inner current is not consulted. It is your individual flow, within the flow of life, all life. This insight grants you access to knowledge that is beyond the scope of your physical senses and is an invaluable source to any area of life to which it is applied.

The notion of communication in this area is essential. It can appear as flashes of insights. It can appear as a sudden urge, or a strong feeling within the body. It can appear as a total opposite idea to what you have been considering. Being in tune with your body is what allows this level of communication to ring through. What is required is simple quiet time. To sit quietly and relax, exploring each and every inch of your body with your awareness, eyes closed, hands on your thighs, palms up and allow yourself to fall into the deep recesses of your body is an exercise that, if done consistently, will cultivate this sensitivity. This will allow you to sense and feel changes in the movement and flow of your body when information is present.

Truly igniting the fire of the body involves realizing that every single occurrence outside of you is connected in some way to your being. The core of your beliefs, thoughts, and emotions are constantly exerting their power and influence on your life. They are placing you in alignment with experiences that are to be.

Purpose

The sword of purpose is easily found hidden in the past of the adult individual. This powerful weapon is found in the areas of life where you find the most pleasure. It is found in the areas in life where you find the most joy. It is often found in those areas of life that come to you most naturally and freely, areas in which, with little effort, you perform well.

Here is where you can find your purpose, a powerful tool that will open the flood gates of exhilaration, personal power and energy, drive and determination. The huge misfortune and sacrifice of the human race is that they have given into the weakness of assuming that another will remain loyal to them in providing their sustenance, the energy of money to fuel their lives and support their family. The organization of big business robbed humans of their creativity, their self-reliance, and their ability to look within for immense inner strength and ability to overcome obstacles and provide for themselves.

If you know where to look, your purpose will be obvious and evident. It will be in line with your highest values and it will bear witness to your most high and inner need to express yourself and expand.

The challenge that you run into after finding your purpose is how to go about expressing yourself through it. Is there a field or position in which you can fully express yourself or must you create a field, a position, or a service?

Timing

The importance of timing is often overlooked in such a fast paced society. The ability to have so many things now, from information to food, we forget that life does not unfold at the push of a button.

Timing requires patience. It requires a mental focus that sustains itself even when things appear to be going awry.

The timing of life is impeccable. When the undercurrent of your life is soaked in LOVE UNCONDITIONAL, you do not have to worry whether the unfolding events of life are in your favor or have your best interest in mind. There is no greater power or appreciation than knowing that you are in control of the flow of your life. The habitual show of emotion that you present to the world is your undercurrent. The *feel* and nature of the people, events, and circumstances in your life are merely a reflection of your inner nature, and this *feel* can slow down or speed up the flow.

If you have begun the exercises within your body, you will have recognized that Love, Joy, Appreciation, Excitement are all high, fast energies that move swiftly and charge the body. Information moves quickly across this energy. Insight moves quickly across this energy, and most importantly the materialization of desired events and circumstances in your life move quickly because of this energy.

On the other hand, you can also feel the energy of anger, frustration, resentment, and hate within the body. It is a destructive energy that destroys or breaks down effort, communication, and relationship.

Escaping the Masses

To escape the mass confusion and intimate relation from pain and suffering one must completely disregard, disavow and dislocate themselves from the thinking of the masses.

You are Entitled…

In some way shape or form the individual human being must turn off or separate from the many inputs that create the noise that keeps him or her from hearing the inner self. These inputs are also what continuously sow seeds of despair, poverty, scarcity, and destruction into one's life.

Everything that tells you what life is and how life is. Everything that serves to keep you from understanding and knowing your majesty, that you are royalty, that anything and everything you desire is already yours, is achievable and available.

Life is merely an enormous verse of potentiality. When you leave your home, you have no idea what circumstances you will meet. You have no clue what people you will meet or how they will behave. The only thing you have control over is your thinking, your intention, the beliefs you carry, and the way you feel.

Pardon me if I say here that this is not only what guides you, but it is what stakes your claim into a certain type of experience. The way you experience life within your mental framework, non-physically, is the way you will experience life within your outer framework, physically.

This is the solid truth that escapes you.

Quantum Physics displays through experiment that you cannot separate what is observed in experimentation from the observer because the mental capacity of the observer impacts the experiment and what they see. Measurable mental activity influences the particles of life on a subatomic level, and these particles are the building blocks to experience. They are the potential brought into solid experience by thought.

Psychology has studied behavior and mind for many years. It has studied how individuals with multiple personalities, through the same body, exhibit distinctly different levels of thinking, feeling, and behaving. All through the same mind and body.

The major spiritual texts of the world, although they come from various teachers, all point out that to connect to the Source of your being, you must work inwardly.

Turning off the noise requires spending quiet time, alone with yourself. It requires that you begin studying and becoming acutely aware of your thoughts, emotions and behaviors, and how most often they are merely automatic responses. They are knee jerk reactions to life. They are reactions whose seeds have been sewn a long time ago. In most areas you no longer think or are aware of whether your emotion and behavior are going to have positive or negative repercussions for you, but everything does.

Your reactions to life do not negate the fact that your thinking is the cause, and no matter how fast the cycle goes, the cause of its turn is not outside of you, it is inside of you.

Touching Base

To finally touch down to the base of your being is to find a calm inner peace no matter what the situation or circumstance that lay before you.

To finally touch the base of your being is to train the mind the think only on those possibilities that you deem worthy of you.

To finally touch the base of your being is to only focus on the life you envision and desire, giving no energy to what may be your present experience.

These are the simple truths that you have always had access to, simple truths, possibilities and abilities that you have always been capable of.

You can think what and how you want to think. You can feel what and how you want to feel in any and every situation. You can be in control of yourself, starting today, and control circumstances, control experiences. You can control what type of people you meet. You can control the type of help you receive. You can control when and

17

how the regular normal occurrences of life happen to and around you. All of these things are within the broad scope of your power, but you must begin claiming the inner responsibility that has always been in front of you.

The Torch of Acceptance

Accepting who you are now – all of your past victories and defeats, all of your successes and failures – is the prerequisite to moving forward in your life. To receive first the knowledge and wisdom that will assist you in burning away the ideas that control you, you must accept the 'you' that you are right now. All events leading up to this point in your life have been (1) necessary for your advancement, growth and expansion; (2) have been created by you and the ideas that you presently hold in your mind about life and the people that exist around you.

What do you believe to be true?

Are people honest and good or are they disrespectful and undeserving? Are you worthy of success or are you destined for failure? Does life conspire to give you what you want, does it conspire to withhold what you want and need, or does it have any influence what so ever? Are the circumstances of your life within your control or out of your control? Does your responsibility extend beyond you or does it rest with you?

Whatever you determine to be true for you is only true because you believe it so. Nothing in life is set in stone because you are the creator. You are the creator of your life. You exist as an inseparable extension of the whole. You exist as a living piece and parcel of that which created the uni-verse and you have been endowed to create your life as you believe and expect it to be, and nothing can stand in the way of your belief and expectation.

That which is the Source of all things is you, and you are it, you are one.

This is what makes everything possible. It is what makes you possible and it extends through you, through your mind into your life only as much as you believe is possible.

So where to go from here?

Only as far as you can see, in your mind. Only as high as you can soar, in your mind. Only as big as you can believe, in your mind. These are your limits.

The chasm that separates the level of achievement of one from the level of achievement of another is the extent of their belief. It is what their current mental system and programming allows them to see and believe.

This is the only difference in human beings, their mental capacity.

Inwardly, each human body, its anatomy, is the same. The only difference from one person to the next is the mental make-up of a subjective mind. A mind that is at the mercy of repeated thought and experience, a mind that does not understand or differentiate between what is physical reality and what is only mental reality.

Ironically, the one that most believe is true is not. Your mental reality is truer than your physical reality, first and foremost because you are not a physical being. You are a non-physical being having a physical experience for a very brief period, an indefinite period of time, and every time you imagine, envision or begin to formulate a life different from the one you currently experience, you subtly begin the process of change. This change becomes evident as the people, who enter your life, begin to change. The opportunities that you come in contact with are of a different nature, and matching resources in the form of information and ideas begin to appear. It is all very obvious if you are aware of what is and does happen. It is the nature of the process for every individual human being's life.

You are Entitled...

The Task

The task that we each are charged with is to build a life and a world of Love and Encouragement, no matter the level. You exist as and to be the full expression of Source within you and that expression can be as a homeless person, a parent, a friend, a business owner, an organization leader, or the leader of nations. No matter the level on which you exist, you can be a beacon of Love and Encouragement.

This does two things.

1. You charge the world around you with your light and other human beings become awakened to the possibility for Love and Joy based on their own creation.
2. You shield yourself from the negative energy that is inherent in the universe by dictating and choosing the type of energy, thought and emotion, that you present.

What you sow comes back to you.

It is not true that there is something you should be doing. You do not have to do anything to be worthy of the ABUNDANCE, LOVE, AND JOY that is available to all. Nature experiences it without choice. The flower does not have to fall to its knees. The honey bee does not leave its home to go worship.

All exists and is ever present.

The blessed gift of the human being is the ability to think. The ability to discern between the two naturally flowing energies of the world. These energies are depicted in many ways around the world, even given physical persona, but the simple truth is that you are merely talking about energy and the ability to discern between the two. This is what makes the human experience so much richer and sweeter.

If there was no bad you wouldn't know what good was. If there was no ugly you would not know what beautiful was. If there was no high there would be no low. If there were no beginning there would be no end.

All serve their purpose, however they are beautiful constructs of the mind and can serve to bind the being who does not at some point move beyond their ability to think into consciously thinking and controlling the mind.

When you begin to think consciously, to choose your thoughts, while creating your beliefs, manipulating your experiences to what you want them to be, you begin to see that the diverse, intricate ability of the mind to separate through choice of perspective is a trap in itself.

To choose a perspective is to separate yourself from one another. To choose a perspective is to deem someone or something less than or greater than another.

The flower that appears less than blessed in color and shape through the eyes of man is no less a flower and blissfully magnificent in its own right in the eyes of its Source.

The tree in the swamp that looks of death and despair is not less beautiful and worthy of sunshine in the eyes of its Source.

The human being, deformed, charred from burn, and angry at life is no less deserving of Love than the new born baby.

Because we choose and allow perspective to guide us it never becomes obvious that the deeper view into life is to LOVE UNCONDITIONALLY.

This removes separation. It allows peace. It carries true insight because there are no mental conceptions or expectations that hinder understanding.

Even the most heinous criminal can do nothing to remove himself or herself from a mother's love. Therefore, there is nothing that you can do to remove yourself from the UNCONDITIONAL LOVE of your Source.

You are Entitled…

To reclaim your life at the deepest level, begin to cultivate LOVE UNCONDITIONAL for your fellow man/woman. If you are moved inwardly by outbursts of anger, disrespectful natures, political, religious, or sexual orientation, you have not attained the UNCONDITIONAL LOVE of Source, and your inner concepts, ideas and expectations continue to bind you.

Free yourself of the trappings of the mind. You have seen and partaken of the separation that exists, and you have taken it in for its season. Now grow to a new, higher level of being, a grander existence by seeing the world through the eyes of your Source. See the world and all of its participants through the eyes and a heart that LOVES UNCONDITIONALLY, and watch the changes that appear in your individual experience.

Common Place

The common ground, the inescapable soil of everyone that lives is that you reap what you sow. This is Law stated in its own way around the world. It is spoken of in terms of cause and effect, and karma. These are all the same. *You Reap What You Sow*, and the sowing is not your physical activity. It is your mental and emotional activity. The roller coaster of life, its highs and lows, ups and downs, good and bad breaks are all the result of a mind that dips, turns, and whips at will, without any guidance or direction.

The curving, winding road that lies in front of most people is the result of a mind that only reacts to the circumstances that it encounters in its outer physical existence. This is the reason for all rules and regulations that presently exist. They are the results of reactions to life, reactions to behaviors and actions that were out of alignment with the true nature of Source. These are the result of choice. These are the result of the choice to exist within the lower levels of energy instead of the higher levels of energy.

When I speak of energy you already know what I mean. You experience them everyday when the various forms of emotion charge your body. Excited, joyous, exhilarating emotion or energy that is produced by you is a very high, very fast moving, very fast flowing energy. Anger, frustration, jealousy, resentment are all low, slow moving energies. Think of the voice tone and quality, the body posture and movements of someone who is depressed. They are in a very low energy state. A state that is not conducive to high level thoughts or solutions. Their state is one of problem focus, *victimhood*, lack of control, and regret. The higher forms of energy are the energies that open doors, create opportunity, and really charge a room.

All energies are contagious, meaning they can be transferred from one person to another. You have all felt the energy of another human being when they were excited or when they were angry.

When you generate any type of energy, you send it, present it out into the universe, and it along with your thoughts and beliefs combine into experience. They combine to form very specific experience and they create the nature of experience.

Angry persons meet angry type experiences in their life. Happy, joyous people meet happy, joyous situations in their lives. It all makes sense, but do not stop at it intellectually, try it for yourself. Decide the type of energy you want to present over a few days and see what you get back. Try the highest energy of Love, and then the lowest of anger. The results will be quite alarming.

The reason we do not know all of this already is that most human beings live somewhere in the middle. Their inner world consists of highs and lows of emotion and thought; therefore, their experiences in life reflect that. The immense numbers of people attaining this type of experience makes it appear normal.

There is better. There is higher.

Just as this nature, your present way of thinking and feeling has been cultivated over time and has become normal, habitual; a higher nature, way of thinking and feeling or attaining to higher levels of consciousness is also possible.

You are Entitled...

As it stands, your challenge is that the cultivation of a higher level of consciousness is not just a mental exercise. It is one that involves the entire body. The body releases chemicals in relation to the emotion that you generate on a regular basis. These chemicals find resting places all through the body and affect the body for better and for worse. Higher states of energy cause the body to release what is called endorphins. Endorphins are healthy chemicals that serve to assist and build the body. The lower forms of energy, anger and depression cause the body to release anti inflammatory agents which are necessary in a fight or flight type situation. These agents, when released over prolonged periods, begin to break down the body and weaken the immune system.

Once a person chooses to remain or cultivate a specific type of thinking and feeling (emotion), the body develops receptors for these chemicals and in a sense becomes an addict for these chemicals, forcing you to go in and out of these mental and emotional states. The end results of habits. You thought habits were only the activities that we as human beings performed outwardly.

Habits are performed inwardly. Thought, emotion and chemical releases are the formative tools to every type of habit from overeating, to overindulgence on sex, to fast driving, to all your behaviors. This is your life, and to change, improve, or cultivate a new one you must begin to challenge those inward processes with conscious thinking (choice), conscious feeling/emotion (choice), and conscious behaviors (choice). This is how you will tell the story as you begin to notice yourself and the events around you begin to mold into the nature of that which you are choosing.

The Destructive

There has always been a destructive link between all who fail to succeed and accomplish that which is their deepest desire. The negative energy of the uni-verse, out of balance in the being that is a human's life is a destructive power to say the least. It breaks relationship between husband and wife, between children and parent, father and son, mother and daughter. It destroys the body, and causes the loss of jobs. It causes bad situations to turn worse. It causes pain and destruction, not just in the wielder but in everything in that person's path, and the intensity of its presentation is the gauge of the damage that it causes.

This negative energy is all yours. You are the chooser. You are the generator. You are the one who presents it to the world and the uni-verse. You have chosen consciously or unconsciously to allow this energy to be your guide and it does its job, serves its purpose with swiftness and decisiveness.

The challenge with this energy is that it is highly contagious, and sets itself apart from all others because of its highly volatile nature.

Very quickly and easily, it also builds a need for repetition within the body. At times it feels like strength. However, being destructive, its source is fear and within the human nature and the physical existence, its presence serves to tear down and not to build or repair.

Is this energy guiding your life? How do you respond when situations that are not of your liking enter into your existence? Does the negative energy of life guide and direct your thoughts, emotions, and behaviors? If so, you should not wonder why negative events appear in your life. It is because your experience matches the energy you present into the uni-verse.

The energies of Source naturally balance themselves in the uni-verse, and in the world or on the planet Earth. However, there is no such balancing mechanism present within the individual human life experience. There is only the choice of which type of energy will be adhered to, and this energy ultimately dictates the types and nature of experience any one being who is human will have.

The culprit of your life is that you are the chooser. You are the generator of the power that fuels your experience. This is why the spiritual wisdoms of the world stress a pure heart, righteousness. This places you solely in the higher energies of the uni-verse, and this is what saves you physically and non-physically from the energies present on both sides of the veil.

25

You are Entitled...

The Veil

Life and death are merely transitions of the being who is human. Because the physical mind does not remember prior transitions, every time it occurs it remains a shock but it is absolutely normal. The veil exists as a separating point between the physical and the non physical realities. It exists to separate the experience of physical life from the higher non physical realities. To wonder what is beyond death is to wonder about the understandings and knowledge that exist within the soul that does not sleep and does not die. To wonder what is beyond the veil is to wonder the truth of who you are and where you come from. This is normal because your being calls to itself constantly for wisdom and knowledge. Your being calls to itself for understanding into the many mishaps and misconceptions, the traumas of life that are not fulfilling dreams or highest desires. This call, when the questions are asked is what awakes the sublime, supreme in you to assist in governing the mind that has taken on its own life.

The problem is that most do not know what they have access to within themselves. They do not know what is there. They do not know that they can experience themselves beyond the veil and change their whole perspective on life.

You, the reader, experience yourself beyond the veil every time you realize you have dreamed. This experience is beyond the mind and beyond the body. You speak to yourself in your dreams and this communication is beyond words.

If you have ever felt trapped in a dream and trying to get out, attempted to force yourself to wake up and heard the body jump and make groaning sounds, you were beyond the veil and can experience this natural position at will with understanding and/or training.

It all serves to empower your understanding of your physical existence and what you are capable of experiencing through your own inner faculties because the power you wield non-physically is your true power and your true self. Non physical you will return to. Non-physically, in truth, you exist right now.

The Deterrent

The deterrent to so many dreams and inwardly inspired notions are the concepts, ideas, and events of the past. These are the blocks that stall any advancement in life.

So let's evaluate these blocks that are lodged away in your unconscious. First you have all of the fears doubts and worries of your parents. At the present moment, your life is the sum total of what your parents were successfully able to accomplish. This is what you saw. This is what you believe is possible. The only way your life experience is drastically different is if you were able to get close enough to someone who had accomplished more, and taken on what they believe to be true and possible. This is where and how our minds get stretched to new possibility.

What you saw in relationships, what you saw or were told of financial possibilities, what you saw of health, the spiritual accomplishments; these are all that you know, and at present are your limits to bigger, greater, and more.

I doubt that the calling of your soul attains the level of ideas that you currently hold. You feel and know within your heart that you could be more, do more, accomplish more and be of a greater influence. You feel in your heart that many of the areas in your life could and should be better, and you have tried but failed miserably. These are your ideas, the blocks stopping you, quieting the voice within.

That voice speaks to your possibility. It knows no bounds, and this is the cause of the conflict within you. It is the cause of the constant disturbance that rumbles deep within. It is the meeting of the possibility and potential that speaks from within, and the ideas and concepts that lurk just below the surface of your conscious mind that serve as the barriers to unbridled effort towards your goals.

So how do you overcome these barriers? Is it possible or do you just succumb to the limiting beliefs within the mind that were given to you and are not even yours?

You are Entitled...

There is a way out, a way to break free, and it is not merely hoping and wishing that things will get better. It is not praying to a heavenly father to grant you your wish this time, please.

No, the overcoming of false ideas about life and your possibility and potential within that life are your responsibility. It is you who must begin to sow the seeds of that which you are to accomplish in your life and it is you who must follow through with the action necessary to solidify the new beliefs within the unconscious.

First, what do you want to experience? Write it down as specific and detailed as possible. Express it in the most magnificent fashion and as vivid as you possibly can. Engage all of your senses as you can, for your inward reality are the building blocks to your outward experience. This must be followed with as many actions as you can take, which are in alignment with the experience that you desire.

If you want beautiful, loving relationships in your life, you must see that in your mind and you must be that with every fiber of your being.

If you want vibrant health you must see it in your mind and you must be it in your behaviors, emotions, and your thoughts.

If you want abundant finances you must begin seeing, speaking (behaving), feeling, and thinking in ways that place you in alignment with abundant finances.

If you want a deeper spiritual awareness and relationship with your Source you must see it in your mind. You must see a grand friendship, a partnership of expression in and through life.

So what are the ideas that are holding you back? Most are not failing in all areas of their lives although some are. Most are great in one or two areas and terrible in others.

They have great relationships but are broke. They are healthy but have no spiritual connection to their Source and do not know why

28

they always feel unfulfilled. They are wealthy but fail in relationships time after time.

There is no outer power destroying your life or holding you back. They are the blocks, the ideas and concepts in your mind that are your only hindrances.

Focus on what you want. Allow no other thought than the successful completion or accomplishment of your goal to enter your mind. Dwell on its completion and what it will feel like, look like, sound like, smell like, taste like. Who will be there? How will you reward yourself? Who else will be affected by your success and accomplishment? Can you see the surprise, admiration, and gratitude on their faces? This mental activity places your success in the present moment. It builds the energy structure of your ideas, your necessary beliefs that continue to draw the resources required to finally present your desire materialized in the physical world.

There are no big desires or small desires when it comes to your experience. It appears that there are such things as big and small, a lot and a little but in spirit, non physical reality, there is no such thing. There is only your desire and if you believe that it should take a long time to acquire your dream or be successful, then you hinder its materialization.

Have you ever wondered why some things happen fast and some things take a long time to occur? It is because we do not have the weight of what should be and what is and is not possible on all desires.

When we speak of desires we mean any thought or idea on which you focused. This is your asking of the uni-verse or God or Source. There is no grand show needed; no bowing of heads and no shaking of hands. The thoughts on which you focus are your asking, and the more you focus on them the more you build them in your mind and in non physical reality. Once they are constructed in non physical reality it is only a matter of time (physical reality terminology) until it shows as experience.

You are Entitled…

Uncovering the Bridge

The bridge to peace, understanding, and the life that we all want is a definite major turmoil. It is turmoil because so many are caught in what the mind has developed as meaning and interpretation that now the blind are leading the blind.

What is required of you, the individual is LOVE, and you think you know what I mean but you do not.

True LOVE does not condemn. It does not criticize. It does not hold back. It does not taunt. It does not force. It does not push. It accepts. It values. It respects. It encourages. It supports. It empowers. It gives hope. It provides higher standards to aspire to. It is trustworthy. It protects. It inspires. It motivates. It brings together. It does not separate or push apart.

Now, to each his own because we are all on our individual journeys and our personal understanding is limited by the amount of wisdom that we are able to comprehend at the moment, but true LOVE frees you.

It frees you from the ups and down of life. It frees you from the mental constraints that bind. It frees you from dark clouds that currently cast shadows across your life because now you have become a light by allowing true LOVE UNCONDITIONAL to swell and grow through your being.

Do you truly LOVE your children unconditionally or do the expectations of society cloud your judgment and cause you to behave in ways that are detrimental to relationship and emotional growth?

Do you truly LOVE your husband, wife, or partner? Can you LOVE them if their ideas and expectations about life oppose yours? Can you LOVE them if their behaviors appear to fall below your expectation or society's standard?

True LOVE requires a deeper, higher level commitment. It requires a thought process that understands that each human being is where they are mentally, physically, and spiritually for a reason, and to push a person when they are not ready shows your immaturity and unwillingness to accept and allow; and this is not LOVE.

LOVE UNCONDITIONAL allows you to wish someone the best no matter what their short comings or behaviors.

True LOVE UNCONDITIONAL is significantly different from what we as human beings call the emotional love. LOVE UNCONDITIONAL is a state of mind, a full state of being, while the emotional love resides within the bounds of expectation and emotional need, and dissolves when the emotional needs are no longer being met.

The Conquering Spirit

The spirit of the conqueror, the courageous adventurer, is what develops as your self worth and confidence grows, realizing that you are creating your life through your thoughts, emotions, and beliefs.

The conquering spirit is not one of disregard for others. It is not one that breaks the rules, destroys another's will, or in any way damages their dreams.

A conquering spirit is one that has realized about the creation and the cycles of life. It has realized that its ability to focus, and demonstrate an unwillingness to compromise in thinking and feeling is how to manifest that which is necessary for a joyous, successful life.

The conquering spirit dances at the appearance of obstacles. They only serve to heighten the focus, attention, and energy given to the end result, the desired outcome sought by the conqueror.

The conquering spirit knows that all who come into his/her life is a benefit and a lesson. They either serve to bring appropriate and necessary resources or they reveal weaknesses in the armor of the spirit which need to be addressed.

The conquering spirit wishes for all to know their true worth, their true potential, and the possibility that lies before them. However, it cannot force others to understand and to act. It realizes that it can merely be an example to those who understand, hear, and see, and it excites the conquering spirit to assists others in uniting their forces.

Developing a conquering spirit requires courage and confidence. It requires an open mind to begin seeing life happening right in front of you, to begin seeing the materialization of your thoughts and beliefs as experience. It truly is exciting. It is exhilarating. It begs the question why haven't I noticed before? How could family members and others have lived their entire lives without knowing, without realizing?

It is because the mind is fickle. The slightest notion of belief and of what is or is not true or possible shuts out anything else and pulls a sheet over all other possibility. Once you are exposed to a new idea, new possibility, and make it a point to understand, you raise the sheet and allow in new learning, new information, and with that you begin to see more happening in the world around you.

The pleasure was mine to serve you, to work with you on your journey, on the project of your life.

You are entitled to all that you desire because you have been given the ability to think and to generate emotion, and these are the non physical activities that create worlds. You are a part of the whole which is one uni-verse, one song. And the beat by which you choose to live your life resonates out and adds back to the whole, for better or for worse. Choose a song that excites, that beckons others to join in and celebrate their lives, celebrate possibilities. Choose a song that compliments the higher good. Choose a song that supports and empowers your fellow human beings. Sing your song louder and dance harder when you feel your experience going out of line, draw it back with the power of your dance, the focus of your mind, and the symphonic harmony of your music.

The champion knows his goal, radiates winning and success, and separates himself from all the naysayer. Follow this example. Be that which you want to experience, and watch the evidence appear before your eyes.

It is always happening, and YOU make it so.

About Benny

Benny Ferguson Jr., once a weary traveler, feeling completely helpless to life, has suffered paralyzing fear, low levels of self-worth and depression, and contemplated suicide. He has attempted and failed, time after time, to achieve and succeed in his finances, his health, and his personal relationships, but always fell victim to unknown fears, self-sabotaging behaviors, limits and barriers.

His personal struggle culminated in 2005, with him waking up at 1:30 am in an anger rage. He woke up after a fear based dream, similar to the ones he had experienced dating back to elementary school, which forced him into an out-of-body experience. From that point he knew that there was more to life than he had previously been taught and ever knew was possible.

His search for an understanding of who he was, what he was capable of, and how to correct the unknown fears and barriers within, led him to the major spiritual traditions of the world (Teachings of Jesus, Buddhism, Hinduism, The Tao, Islam), branches of Psychology, and to Quantum Physics.

The Result:

"The Diamond Mind Approach to Life and Business,"

Where Benny ventures to explain and help human beings become aware for themselves (REMEMBER), that each individual is creating their own life experience through the images they hold as beliefs (unconsciously), their thoughts and their emotions.

Life is being lived from the inside out, and the moment we begin to live life from this understanding we realize that it is true.

"The Diamond Mind Approach to Life and Business" explains:

Life
- Why and how life is being lived from the inside out;
- How to become aware of your thoughts and their continuous manifestation;
- How to take control of the Core Inner Processes, the nonphysical faculties that are the fundamental starting point to life (beliefs, thoughts, emotions);
- How to begin observing and become aware of the subtle changes, materializations and manifestations, that occur as a result of your inner work;
- How to develop a **Diamond Mind** that does not compromise with life.

Business
- How to manage and take control of the mind of your business or organization;
- How the mind of your business and your employees is sabotaging skill and potential;
- How a **Diamond Mind** frees you and your employees of preexisting programming that hinders approaching maximum performance, production, and potential;
- Why/How no less than a **Diamond Mind** in Leadership, Sales, Customer Service and Organizational Culture should be accepted.

Connecting With Benny:

Facebook: www.facebook.com/bennyrfergusonjr

Youtube: https://www.youtube.com/user/BennyFergusonJr/videos

Twitter: www.twitter.com/BennyRFergusonJ

Contacting Benny:

Initial contacts to Benny for discussions, interviews, one – on - one or group coaching, speaking or training may be made through telephone or email.

Phone: 336-546-7142

Email: BennyFerguson@TheFergusonCompany.com

www.ingramcontent.com/pod-product-compliance
Lightning Source LLC
Chambersburg PA
CBHW021922040426
42448CB00007B/867